A Time For Truth
&
Love

Eric Darnell Boone

Copyright © 2024 by Eric Darnell Boone
All rights reserved.

DEDICATION

This book is dedicated in memory of the late
Alice Alpine Williams Boone, my mother, who died in
July 1985
And the late Susan Williams, my grandmother
Who died in December 1986 leaving this world
With a violent thunder.
I would like to extend my appreciation
To my family, teachers and friends
Who encouraged me in hard times
To write until my life ends.

TABLE OF CONTENTS

CHAPTER 1: Romantic Poems

MEAN ROLLER SCOOTER 2
A TIME FOR ROMANCE 3
PROM NIGHT 4
MY MAIN-SQUEEZE 5
FOREVER LOVERS 6
BY THE SEA OF LOVE 7
THE EXPECTATIONS OF FRIENDSHIP 8
IT'S OVER 9
FORGIVENESS 10
MY LOVE DIVINE 11
FRIENDSHIP COMES 12
DISTANT LOVERS (A SOLDIER AND HIS WIFE) .. 13

CHAPTER 2: POEMS OF LOVE

A SPECIAL MOTHER 16
A BIG-MOUTH SISTER 17
A SPECIAL SISTER 18
A VERY SPECIAL FRIEND 19
MY GRANDMOTHER 20
GOOD FRIENDS 21
A COURAGEOUS PROVIDER 22

HAPPY BIRTHDAY WISE OLD OWL 24
CLOSER TO SHORE 25
A CARING FRIEND 26
IN MEMORY OF MOM AND GRANDMA................ 27
A DEVOTED AUNT 28

CHAPTER 3: POEMS ABOUT MARRIAGE

ANTICIPATION 30
MY WEDDING DAY 31
SMOKING RUINS YOUR MARRIAGE...................... 32
HARD TIMES IN A MARRIAGE 33
UNITED AS ONE 34
ONE BODY... 35
A NEW STEP IN LIFE 36
A SUCCESSFUL MARRIAGE...................................... 37

CHAPTER 4: INSPIRATIONAL POEMS

THE TRUE MEANING OF CHRISTMAS................... 40
BELIEVING IN MYSELF AND JESUS CHRIST 41
GOD IS SUPERMAN 42
ETERNAL LOVE 43
WE LOVE OUR GOD... 44
GOD NEVER FAILS 45
SALVATION 46
A COWARD CHRISTIAN 47
GOD'S GRACE 48
THE GREATEST DAY OF MY LIFE 49
SWEET VICTORY - JESUS IS REAL TO ME............ 51

CHAPTER 5: POEMS ABOUT MY GROWING PAINS, CHAINS OF THOUGHT, AND LIFE EXPERIENCES

I AM 56
CITY BOY 57
CRACKED RAPPERS 58
WHISPERING SPARROWS 59
ATHLETIC DESIRE 60
A SAD JULY 61
A DREADFUL DAY - SATURDAY, JULY 27, 1985 ... 64
A TEMPORARY PAIN-A BEITER TOMORROW 65
FOLLOW THAT SHINING STAR 67
LONELINESS 68
SA YING GOOD-BYE 69
BEING A SOLIDER REQUIRES ENDURING SOME PAIN 70
SECOND PLATOON'S MOTTO 71
ROTC 72
ECHO COMPANY'S MOTTO 73
STRONG LOVE 74
MISTREATED 85
THE KEY TO LIFE 86
BEING SUCCESSFUL 87
INDIVIDUALISM-BEING YOURSELF 88
YOUR CONSCIENCE 89
DEBBIE'S NIGHTMARE 90
DRUGS AND ALCOHOL-THE SILENT KILLERS .. 92
SUICIDE 93
MY LIFE AS IT IS NOW 95

CHAPTER 1:
ROMANTIC POEMS

MEAN ROLLER SCOOTER

I am a mean roller scooter
And I am rolling down the line
I am going to rock your soul
With a little rock and roll.
I am the most talented poet ever known
I am going to keep writing I'm grown
I am going to delight you with my rhymes
Because my poetry continues to shine.
I am going to dazzle your soul
With a little rock and roll.
A Rap

A TIME FOR ROMANCE

A time is given for everything
All the needed help to blossom and grow
There is a special place for everyone
A path where no feet but ours can go.
A time is set aside in which we learn
First is crawl and walk, to run and play
And then the riches and the wiser joys
Are saved for us yet another day.
There is a time for heart-aches and for sighs
A time for laughter and a time for sad songs.
Because God keeps a roll of all deeds
Time for sensational moments to last long
God so ordained that it should be this way.
It knows no reasons, and the time for love
Is yesterday, tomorrow and today.
The things we do will soon be past
Unless we do the things that will last.
The comfort and love
Will last until the eternal end.
Even though we have had
Our joys and pains
My love for you
Will always be the same.
By Eric Darnell Boone & Brenda Diane Cleveland

PROM NIGHT

Boy and girl
Go to Oaks Club
Have lots of fun
And drink some rum.
Because of these passionate moments
Sexual desires have just begun.
They leave real early
To indulge in a romantic dinner
An hour later they arrive
At the Hotel Swinger.
They caress another's body in bed
They are both so hot
Girl saves her virginity by leaving
With boy on the waterbed cot.

MY MAIN-SQUEEZE

She is special and she's fine
I think that she is one of a kind
I was smart in choosing her as my friend
Because she is educated and dedicated
To be with me to the very end.
She is soft and fluffy
Gee, she's too pretty
She looks delicious and Aha so good
I think her for treating me
The way a woman should.
She is my inspirational tower
Oh, so sweet til sour
I want to make love
To her each and every hour.

FOREVER LOVERS

Let me tell you about a book I read
It was so happy it could raise the dead
It's entitled IF BEALE STREET COULD TALK
Then all of the lovers in America would walk.
Refrain: So now they are back together again
Bonded by that insepratable love
That will hold together
Until the end.
Here are my characters in this line
To start it off here is Clementine
She is 19 years old, slim and sleek
With a body build better than a freak
She is so cute, the guys say she is fine
She's a ten, while other girls are a nine
She is so special, Gee yes indeed
She makes all of the guys weak to their knees.
Repeat the refrain!
She is in love with this guy named Lonnie
But people call him Fonny
He is in jail serving some time
For the rap of an untrue crime
He gets out in the very end
By the confession of his friend.
Repeat the refrain!
A Love Rap Song

BY THE SEA OF LOVE

By the sea of love, where we hide
So that we can lay side by side
We are special lovers and we're true
We perk up each other when one is blue
We cherish that wonderful love forever
We share these passionate moments together
Proving that an everlasting bond exists between us
And that our love is stronger than leather
Sweetheart, your body is soft and warm
It is made in the near perfect form
You are gentle and you are cute
Your love is safer than a parachute
Your kisses are so sweet
Your lips are sensitive and tender
I just want to have your love
Every second on my agenda
By the sea of love
Two innocent lovers play in the dark
Caressing each other's sexy body
Creating that long-lasting spark.

THE EXPECTATIONS OF FRIENDSHIP

It is the tiny joys of friendship
That always mean so much
The romantic letters, the frequent visits
That keeps good friends in touch
It is the peaceful understanding
The special times meant for two
The small favors of kindness
Caring friends so often do
It's the little gifts of friendship
The sweet and sharing ways
The caring that adds special flavor
To sour and boring days
What a world of happiness
These little presents can bring
For they start a lasting treasury
Of fond remembering.
By Eric Boone & Linda Moss

IT'S OVER

It's over and this is the end
Now she is not even my friend
I gave her my best
But it wasn't good enough
I devoted all of my time
To giving her the luxuries of life
I gave her my umbrella in the rain
I was her maid when she was in pain
It hurts deeply to have a companion
That rejects and leaves one after
All of the ups and downs
Resounding now I ask the Lord
For his healing touch
To help me forget
About that friend
Whom I loved so much.

FORGIVENESS

I miss that sense of touch
I realize now, I love you so much
I miss your tender loving care
I miss running my hands through your hair
Honey, I miss you holding me
In your arms real tight
I miss making love to
You all through the night
I am sorry, I am sorry
I never meant to hurt you
Please forgive me of living
And speaking the untrue
No one that struts this soil is perfect
Mistakes have been and will always be made
I suffer dearly in my saddened heart
Because my wrong-doings have been painfully paid
Let's goon with our lives
By sharing these tingling moments together
Honey, would you please take me back
I come humblely pleading like an unsupported shack.

MY LOVE DIVINE

You're like a lemon sherbet
Nice, yellow, gentle and sweet.
I love you from the depth of my heart
I know that our friendship will never depart.
Brenda, you have never failed me
And have always stood by my side
In my soul I cherish your love
Where it will always abide.
You are like the sunshine
That brightens up my day.
You bring out the best in me
So that I am special in every way.
You are beautiful
Your appearance is real neat
I thank you for your love
Every day of the week.
I just want to reward you
With these words of joy
Because Brenda you're a great friend
And you are true
Have an exciting day
And remember I love you!

FRIENDSHIP COMES

Friendship comes
When the attraction of man and woman is displayed.
Friendship comes
When two people share
Another's likes and dislikes.
Friendship comes
When partners share
Each other's ups and downs.
Friendship is started
When two strangers extend
Their hands in love.
Friendship comes
When you have a shoulder
To weep on.
Friendship comes
When you have someone to pass
A handkerchief to wipe your watery eyes.
Friendship is here
When one is feeling unwanted and blue
A caring person shares a candy and smiles at you.

DISTANT LOVERS (A SOLDIER AND HIS WIFE)

My lover is not here
For times I feel alone
But I remember that my darling
Is just a few miles from me at home
When we meet together we express our love
Darling, your body is as soft as a dove
Darling, please touch me all over
And let me hold you in my arms real tight
I want to make you feel like a woman
By making love to you all through the night
When she have came and left
I feel wonderful and wanted again
She is a great lover and she is true
My distant lover I am crazy about you.

CHAPTER 2:
POEMS OF LOVE

A SPECIAL MOTHER

Morn, you're our counselor and our teacher
But most of all you're our preacher.
You are special that you are
You're like the beautiful sea breeze so far.
I know that you love us
And we love you too
That's why we try to do
Everything that is commanded by you.
May God continue to bless you each and every day
May he continue to guide you along straight pathway
May God bless you today in his own special way
Mom, Happy, Happy Mother's Day.

A BIG-MOUTH SISTER

To a big-mouth sister, who always
Has got something to say
To a big-mouth sister, who brightens
Up my gloomy days.
Barbara you are one of a kin'd
I thank the Lord for.my friend divine
You're so sweet
And you are truly neat.
You're a great sis that you are
You're like the light that brightens the star.
And to this big-mouth sister
Who that is special in every way
I want to give you this tiny gift
Expressing my love
And say Happy St. Valentine's Day
And remember I love you.

A SPECIAL SISTER

To a kind sister
Who cheers me up when I cry
To a caring sister
Who makes a great apple pie
To a beautiful friend
Who is always there
To a caring sister
With silky black hair
To a caring person
Who prevented me from being bad
To a special friend
Who talks to me when I am mad
Michelle, you are pretty
And you dress real neat
You're very special
And truly sweet
I just want to reward you
With a few lines of love
Because you're a special sister
And you are true
Have a Happy Birthday
And remember I love you.

A VERY SPECIAL FRIEND

You are a special friend, Oh yes Sheba
Because you're there in my times of want
You are like the rainbow
You brighten up my day.
You're loving, witty, understanding
And you are always more demanding ..
You encourage that light in me
To shine Aha so clear
So that people can see
That I am important, and is seldom free.
You're my friend today today and tomorrow
I know that you will not let me drown in my sorrow.

MY GRANDMOTHER

My grandmother Susan Williams is fun
To have and be around
She will sit talking about the good old days
By describing what really went down.
My Granny is the key
She is the light of my work!
She tells me bedtime stories
And gives me a candy squirl.

GOOD FRIENDS

These good friends have always
Stood by our side
And help us attain
The things we need.
Our dependable friends are
Intelligent and understanding
These are special friends
Who answer our every plead.

A COURAGEOUS PROVIDER

(A story of Illusion)

All over the world, the father is known as the head of the family whose responsibility is to provide for his family with the necessities and luxuries of life. It was 10 a.m. on Christmas Eve, 1975, and my father was away from home on a quest for money, because he had been unemployed or eighteen months and his unemployment compensation had ceased. The reason Daddy was on his quest was to purchase gifts, so that his family could have a joyous holiday. Poppa called home and told the family, "do not worry, because I will be home tomorrow with the gifts."

Dad traveled through the suburb and the forest for because of this heavy traveling Dad was tired and hungry. He stopped at several houses and asked, "if they had any leftovers that could be shared with him?" The house owners replied, "'No, get lost, bum." These acts of unkindness did not stop Dad from his venture. Although he was tired and hungry, Pop continued on until he reached an unattended pecan and pear orchard in the forest, where he ate and drank from the sprinkler.

After Poppa had finished eating and drinking, he continued his expedition until he arrived in town. Within the next eight hours, Daddy was refused employment by twenty hotels, five motels and two discos. He went into a bar and asked for work. The owner replied, "no!" Dad walked for an hour to reach a logging company, where he asked for work and was also refused.

These disappointments, however, didn't discourage Dad from his quest. He continued until he arrived at a farm where the farmer needed help. Dad walked away, the job was different from what he expected. The farmer's wife observed Poppa's actions, so she asked him, "how would he like to win a car, a sixty pieces box of fried chicken, a ham, a turkey, and ten thousand dollars for staying on a wild bull for nine seconds?" Dad answered, "yes, ma' am." She took Poppa to the rodeo and paid his entrance fee. Several contestants got their chances to ride the bull, but failed.

It was now Poppa's turn to ride the bull. Dad rode the bull for 11 seconds - allowing him to take home the gifts. Daddy received his gifts, thanked the farmer's wife for taking him to the rodeo and paying his entrance fee, left the rodeo, and arrived home by 6 a.m. on Christmas morning. He woke us up and showed us the gifts. Poppa was successful in bringing home the bacon. Daddy, our courageous provider, also led the family in fellowship thanking the Lord for his blessings. The family ate dinner together and we had a joyous holiday.

A FICTION

HAPPY BIRTHDAY WISE OLD OWL

Hello there wise old owl
Let me hear you howl
Happy Birthday to you
Because you will never see 22.
May this day be lived
With all of life's greatest excitements
Living life to its extent
From one of your dedicated fans
May your mailbox be jammed
Packed with the many presents.

CLOSER TO SHORE

You should be happy today
Because you're one year older
Wiser and free.
Today is your day
You are recipient of many gifts
And even a money tree.
Happy Birthday Daddy
May you live to see many more
Watch your step by being careful
Because you're one step closer to old man shore.

A CARING FRIEND

You're never too busy to listen
When troubles or problems appear
You're always on hand
With a word or a smile.
You're someone that cares
Who is nice to be near.
Guess that's why
You're somebody special
And why you're remembered
This way.
With the fond thoughts
And many wishes
As well.
Thank you for your love
That's why you are my friend
"Caring Friend"
Yes that is true
I want you to have a lovely day.
By Eric Boone and Valerie Croker

IN MEMORY OF MOM AND GRANDMA

(Mother's Day, May 10, 1987)
The thrill of buying a queen
A gift has gone
But I can recall to memory effortlessly
The teachings and goals left reminiscing on
Mothers and grandmothers are stubborn preachers
They are coaches of the great
They're the night stalkers
And fixers of the plate
When one is sick
Feeling Oh so bad
Mom and Grandma enters with a cup of cocoa
Smiling, wearing that bright pretty plaid
We can chat for days
And days or years or years
Of what Mom and Grandma wanted me to be
They brought me to Jesus Christ
And told me how I could be free.

A DEVOTED AUNT

My dear sweet supportive friend
Who is my attractive aunt
You are my consolation
Through the nightmare jitters of haunt
There are numerous imagery appointed you
So many that I am unaware to start
Your love has inspired in me anew
That sense of touch soothing my heart
Annie Mae, your shining flare of light
Has guided me along that shallow pathway
Here are some soft spoken words expressing my love
"I love ya" this sunny day.

CHAPTER 3: POEMS ABOUT MARRIAGE

ANTICIPATION

The most exciting
Nerve-wracking day
Of our lives.
A
N
T
I
c
I
p
A
T
I
0
N
ON OUR WEDDING DAY
When me and my special friend
Will join in holy wedlock
By becoming husband and wife.

MY WEDDING DAY

Floating through the spring breeze
I searched the land of gold
Looking for that special companion
That was love-sick bold
I traveled many miles
Climbing high hills and deep valleys
With determination to cross the Nile
Where my companion was in a sacred alley
My companion and I met
In this large unfriendly site
We based our relationship
On love, trust, and true light.
We praised our Father for his blessings
For providing me with my suitor
Waiting on the dock
For Christ's love and power
We thanked our Heavenly Father
For this very beautiful day
Celebrating the marriage of my wife and Christ to me
On this the tenth day of May.

SMOKING RUINS YOUR MARRIAGE

Tonight is a very special night for you and me
Angela, would you please marry me
So that we can share my millions of dollars together.
Angela, says yes and lights up a cigarette
Begins smoking, blowing the smoke into my face
I get mad stomps my feet and snatch the cigarette
From out of her mouth and tells her
"It's over between us
And you are not going to get a dime
Because I don't want a wife
Who smokes all of the time."

HARD TIMES IN A MARRIAGE

The marriage life is filled
With ups and downs
Because it often seems like
Someone wants to sit around.

UNITED AS ONE

A relationship based on two ideals
Is unable to stand.
But a marriage based on one ideal
Will be able to withstand
The rain, wind, and sand.
I would sacrifice the pain
By not receiving the fame
Because I have your love
And that is all I need
We are the winners of the game.
A marriage that doesn't contain
The presence of God
Is like an interstate with a big hole.
Inviting God into your marriage
And by obeying his commandments
Keeps partners in control.

ONE BODY

Now united as one
We sleep as one
We eat as one
We make love as one
We suffer as one
We share our finances as one
We celebrate as one
We do everything together as one
And we thank our Father for
The birth of our first son.

A NEW STEP IN LIFE

Marriage is an intricate step
Sometimes it is one that you might regret
But if Jesus is represented as uno
Then this would be the most rewarding help.

A SUCCESSFUL MARRIAGE

To have a successful marriage
These are the things that you must do
You must be true to your partner
And your partner must be true to you.
Therefore, your house must serve
The Lord in a Christian manner
Uplifting his name and by thanking him
For his many blessings
And the Lord will place you marriage
On a silver banner.

CHAPTER 4: INSPIRATIONAL POEMS

THE TRUE MEANING OF CHRISTMAS

Almighty and everlasting God
We thank you Father for your many blessings.
Have mercy upon us and instill in our hearts
The true meanings of Christmas.
Help us Father to remember that
Christmas is the season of giving and sharing
But for some it is the time of begging.
The holiday season of Christmas is recognized
As the time of celebrating the joys of life.
The celebration with family and friends
Eating, drinking, and opening our new things.
For some individuals there will be no gifts
Because they will be suffering from bereavement
Pains, financial difficulties, lack of food or a home
And also some people will be left all alone.
Father, help us to realize that
The true meanings of Christmas are to
Celebrate the birthday of your son
By dedicating our lives to him
And to help the needy by giving food, money, clothing
And also to express our love by sharing and caring. Amen.

BELIEVING IN MYSELF AND JESUS CHRIST

I will believe in myself
For there is nothing I can't accomplish
I will work hard each and every day
With Jesus leading me in the narrow pathway.
I will-be the best
In everything I do
Let me be above the rest
Skying over you.
So, as I labor, thirst, and sweat
Help me Christ to wear my goal oriented vest.
I will work hard every second of my life
It will be said, "I was the man named Mr. Strife."

GOD IS SUPERMAN

God is my superman
For he is where ever I go
God is my light and my salvation
So whom shall I be afraid of.
God has never made a mistake
Besides he's always on time
When one is out in the dangerous wilderness
And lost all alone
Superman will pick you up
God will carry you back home.

ETERNAL LOVE

I wanted eternal love
I found it in the wind
I met this courageous stranger
I found her as my friend
So we met in heaven
Where friendships never end.
In the almighty heaven
We roamed the streets of gold
Dressed in white like angel doves
Spreading that eternal love
Because we are leaning on God
Where we have an everlasting hold.

WE LOVE OUR GOD

We love our God
For he first loved us
We will uplift his name
By giving him our trust
God assured us that he is our friend
He will be at our sides
In times of sickness
Hard-aches and pains
He is our shelter in the rain
God will be with us through the end
God has protected us
Every second of each day
He promises to be beside us
And not let us go astray.

GOD NEVER FAILS

God never fails
I can see his work applause
He is our deliverer
No matter what's the cause.
I never worry
I never fret
Because God Almighty
Has never failed me yet.
Though I have been beaten
Hated and rebuked
I have also been burned and stoned.
I never worry because
God said
"I will never leave my child alone."

SALVATION

In my Father's house
There are many mansions
Rubies, diamonds, silver, and gold
I want to be a child of the King
Where ever I go
Let me hide in thee
Putting in him my trust
Let me go abound
And witness without lust
It would profit
A man of nothing
To gain the many mansions
And let his soul be lost
Believe, confess, and ask the Lord
To become the head of your life
He will step in and save you
It's really easy
He has already paid the cost.

A COWARD CHRISTIAN

A coward Christian is ashamed of God
He is afraid of what men might say
He is so, so ashamed that
He won't kneel down to pray
A coward Christian is afraid to stand up
For what he believes is right
He is even afraid to clap hands
And give God the praise tonight
A coward Christian is always fearful
Forever feeling blight
He is also afraid of singing the Lord's song
And speaking the truth and light.

GOD'S GRACE

Heavenly Father, Heavenly Father
Without you nothing can be!
You are mighty and you are able
To guide us as we travel along
This Christian journey each and every day!
We are asking for your strength, guidance ,
And protection as we sojourn along our way
Help us Lord that we will do
What's pleasing in the sight of you!
Father, we want to do the best
Of what we're assigned to
So that we can say that
Father, we have done what you told us to do. Amen.

THE GREATEST DAY OF MY LIFE

I was at Easter Sunday morning service
With my mother, two sisters, and brother
I had read by Bible regularly
I knew how to get saved
But I waited for this glorious day
The day of truth ·
Had finally at last approached
I remembered that Bible verse which states
With Jesus saying
"Suffer the little children to come unto me
For such is the kingdom of heaven.
Whosoever that doesn't enter the kingdom of God
As a child, one shall not enter there in." LUKE 18:16
I was sitting at the back of the church
The late Rev. Abraham Gadsden, our pastor
Opened the doors of the church
Asking if anyone would like
to give their life to Jesus.
I wanted to go and be saved
But Satan was working wonders
Without those butterflies in my stomach
so I decided not to go.
Our pastor kept reading Bible verses
And extending the invitation to come to Jesus.
I listened to the choir singing "Just as I am
without one plea, the blood of the Lamb was shed for me

0 Lamb of God, I come"
The seat that I was sitting became hot
Then my whole body became extremely hot.
Then my whole body became extremely hot.
Jesus spoke to me and said, "Come to me!"
I ranged walked up to the altar, shake hands with the pastor
I asked the Lord to forgive me of my sins
I confessed to the Lord that I was a sinner
I believed that the Lord is Savior of the world
And he would save me.
So I became saved at 12:45 p.m. on Easter Sunday, 1978
In Redeemer Reformed Episcopal Church in Pineville, S.C.
I feel great today
Because I am a Christian at 11 years old.
I have turned over a new leaf
I was once on the brown side
Outside looking in
But now I am on the green side
Celebrating salvation with Christ my friend.

SWEET VICTORY - JESUS IS REAL TO ME

Chorus 1.
Sweet victory, sweet victory
Jes-us is so real
Sweet victory, sweet victory
He always makes a good deal
Sweet victory, sweet victory
Jes-us is so real
Sweet victory, sweet victory
He provides us with a meal.
Nearly two thousand years ago
Jesus appeared on this earth
God fulfilled his prophecy
By releasing his son from heav-en
He sent him to repent, repent-bassers repeat
This whole wide sinful world
Answering the cries of sinners
By saving our dreadful souls.
Repeat Chorus 1.
(break it down) Chorus 2.
Sweet victory, sweet victory
Jes-us is so real
He brought me out of captivity
And he has set me free
I tha-nk him for his grace
And his precious liberty

Sweet victory, sweet victory
Sweet Jes-us is good to me.
Repeat Chorus 1.

Neaily two thousand years ago
Jesus appeared on this earth
God fulfilled his prophecy
By releasing his son from heav-en
He sent him to repent, repent-bassers repeat
This whole wide sinful world
Answering the cries of sinners
By saving our dreadful souls.
Chorus3.
Sweet victory, sweet victory
Jes-us is good to us
Sweet victory, sweet victory
He defeats our temptations of lust
Sweet victory, sweet victory
We thank him for his love and power
Sweet victory, sweet victory
He is with us every hour
Sweet victory, sweet victory
Jes-us is good to me
Sweet victory, sweet victory
Jes-us is so real to me.
(break it down) solo
Jes-us is so re-al
He is re-al to me
He is real for I can
Feel him in my soul ,
They whipped, scorned, and terrorized my Savior
Jes-us never said a mumbling word

He shed his blood on Calvary
To save both you and me
I thank God that I am saved
I thank you Jes-s for being so real
So re-al
So re-al
So re-al
So re-al to me
Repeat Chorus 1.
Repeat Verse 2.
Repeat Chorus 3.
A gospel song

CHAPTER 5: POEMS ABOUT MY GROWING PAINS, CHAINS OF THOUGHT, AND LIFE EXPERIENCES

I AM

I am a student at the University of South Carolina.
I am a freshman
I am enrolled in University 101.
lam nice
lam cool
I am a poet too.
I am a song writer
I am a caring individual
I am a gifted person too
I am a hard worker do.
lam a lover
lam big
I am strong
I am an eater of figs
lam fast
I am a teenager
I am the starter of the blast.
I am proud of who I am
I am now a mature man. ,
Listen up let me tell you
Who I be
I am the rising poet. known as E.D.B.

CITY BOY

Slice it
Dice it
Make it sound
Real nice.
If you don't
Want to rock
Go and
Fly a kite.
Refrain: You're growing
With the crew
We're going to shock you
If you're blue.
These are square-headed turks
Known as men called Mr. Jerks
They are not cool
They look like a fool
Walking around town
Strutting in their ballet shoes.
Repeat refrain:
Wow here is to you
All you fine fly girls
Who refuses to listen
]To Mr. Jerks or a fool
Listen up to the city boy
Who invented the word cool.
Repeat refrain
A Rap

CRACKED RAPPERS

Husky boys are whack
Ugly, fat, and blue-black
All of the prostitutes talk about
This rapper Johnny Grow
They say that he isn't a good lover
Besides he is too slow.
Refrain: Look out your window
Glancing at the sexy body of me
I am the upcoming rapper
Known as Flyboy "E."
They talk about this rapper
Named Jerry Mow
His picture was in
The National Enquire rocking
This homosexual named Fast Joe.
Repeat refrain:
You talk about the guys
Named Jump DVC
They are low-down and dirty
That is why their deodorant
Won't agree.
Repeat refrain
A Rap

WHISPERING SPARROWS

Whispering sparrows
Nothing to worry about
Life seems to be
Quiet, peaceful, and pleasant
It is spring once again
So it must go out
And gather new straws, sticks, and weeds
To build its castle.
Their mating season
Begins in March
With the blossoming
Of Easter lilies and buds
A newborn whispering sparrow
Chants the call of early morning
Arriving just in time
To reveal that it is spring.

ATHLETIC DESIRE

In love with hard work
Excessive sweat with painful tears
The athletic desire is to
Give 100% in every play of the game
Theoretically, you could suffer a sudden injury
Ending your career without receiving fame.

A SAD JULY

A month that started off being extremely happy ended up being sad. It was Friday, July 5, 1985, and we were having a small family gathering (Daddy, Momma, Barbara, Michelle, Clifford, Keith and me) and our friends. My brother Calvin was unable to attend because he was on police duty. We sat around playing checkers and cards, singing, preaching, laughing, eating and joking together. Then at 4:30 p.m., Mom saw that we needed some more food, so she went to town to buy some more groceries. While she was away, we continued having a joyous time.

Then at 5:30 p.m., the telephone rang; I picked up the phone, the caller told me that Momma was involved in a terrible car accident. I started crying, then I stumbled into the kitchen and told my family the bad news. Everyone started crying, and screaming; saying, "no, no, no this can't be true!" Finally after two minutes of shock, we all rushed down to the accident in tears. When we arrived on the scene, we saw the car bent in the shape of a ''U" and the Emergency Medical Service squad was trying to cut her out of the car. Mom was in severe pain screaming and begging them: "Please take me out!" All the family could do was cry, pray, and imagine the pain that Mom was suffering. After one hour, they finally removed her from the car. Most of her body was covered with blood, but she was still breathing. The family was relieved because she was alive. The emergency specialists put her inside the ambulance and transported her to the emergency room. The 'family followed the ambulance to the hospital. After we arrived at the emergency room Barbara called Calvin and told him the bad news. Calvin was shocked and started crying. They conversed for thirty minutes and then Calvin hung up. Mom was treated negligently because she was not thoroughly examined, and she was also released in sixty hours following her serious accident.

On Monday, July 8 at 7 a.m., the family went to the hospital and brought Momma home crippled. Her legs were swollen twice their normal size with an open cut one inch deep, she had a broken arm, a cracked rib and most of all, she couldn't stand up by herself. Because she was helpless, we had to do everything for her. I was tired most of the time because I had to take care of Momma and clean the house, while Daddy, Keith, and everyone else were at their jobs.

A week later a false report written by the highway patrolman was printed in our local newspaper about the accident. Mom was charged with failure to yield the right of way, and most importantly the insurance company refused to pay the claim. However, all of these statements were acts of prejudice, because Momma did not cause the accident. It was caused by a drunken driver who made a sudden stop and therefore, forced Mom to slam on the brakes. Since it was raining, the car started skidding and was smashed into by a white man, who was speeding eighty miles per hour.

It was so painful watching someone that you dearly love suffer on their dying bed. Momma continued to get worse each day, although she was going to the doctor two or three times a week. On the morning of Saturday, July 27, 1985 at 8:45 a.m., she collapsed and screamed, "Oh Lord, please help me! I can't take it anymore!" and then she died of internal bleeding. Because of this tragedy, this was indeed "A SAD JULY." It was heart breaking witnessing that the death of a loved one was caused by a doctor's negligence and them is treatment of a highway patrolman, the news media and the insurance company.

A DREADFUL DAY - SATURDAY, JULY 27, 1985

Life has taken a drastic change for me
For part of my life is missing
And I just don't know where it is.
It just seems to be so knife-cutting painful
Part of my life has been cut away
I have this intensive feeling
That my life has also come to an end!
My Mother's death just leaves
A hollow hole in my heart
It's like no other pain
I have felt before!
But at the end of this pain
Is the fact that God has brought
Another one of his servant's life to an end.
God has called her life to depart
Now she eats from the Holy Spirit Pot.
God is merciful in taking her
A way from her suffering
She now resides in heaven
As an angel singing.

A TEMPORARY PAIN-A BEITER TOMORROW

Almighty and everlasting God
The aid of those in need.
I am asking you Father to please
Have mercy upon this family
In their hours of bereavement.
We thank you Father for
Yet another day.
We thank you for all of
Your many blessings.
We thank you Father for ,
The good time sand the bad
And for the wonderful experiences
We and our loved one shared.
This pain that one feels
Is just temporary
Although it seems like
It will last forever!
Father, you promised us
That you will
Help us bear this burden
If we be still.
Father please fill that
Emptiness in our hearts
Because one of our sweet friends
has left and departed!

Father, help us to understand that
no matter how hard life may seem
If we put our trust in you
You will brighten these dark
Days with a gleam.
Father, please bless this family
In their times of sorrow
And help us to realize
There is a better tomorrow! Amen.

FOLLOW THAT SHINING STAR

As sure as one is born
One must die
But if one die in Christ
One will eat heavenly pie
My dear Aunt Blossom was a glow of light
That touched many hearts and shined afar
She was a caring mother, a peaceful, graceful friend
She was indeed a Christian Star.
As a devoted Christian
She worked day and night
Uplifting the Lord's name
By speaking the true light
With all her might
God called her home to receive that just reward
So she is now gone
But she set forth a righteous example of a Christian
That we must carry on.

LONELINESS

My sweetheart is far away
Gosh I miss her dearly
I have to yet face
Another lonely day.
I miss seeing her beautiful face
Along with her brown curly hair
But most importantly I'm saddened by the fact
Of her not being here
She's my light
Her love makes me shine
Father, I miss my partner
Oh Brenda, Brenda divine!

SAYING GOOD-BYE

Saying good-bye is something
That is hard to do
Because you're going to miss
That person that's leaving you
You will miss that person's love
And most of all their care
That's why no one wants to say good-bye
Because they feel that it is so unfair
I want to say good-bye tomorrow
But by then I would be there
-So I am going to say it now
While I am still here
"Good-bye and thank you for
The times that were happy and sad"
"Good-bye and thank you for
The wonderful experiences we had."

BEING A SOLIDER REQUIRES ENDURING SOME PAIN

When the pain starts growing
The Armed Forces keep on going
We are fighting men who obey orders and duties
As soldiers to labor for this country
It is an honor and a challenging
Responsibility for the Armed Forces to protect
This great land from day to day
Fighting to preserve the American way
We are fighting men
Who fight in rain, sleet, or snow
Laboring each and every day
By delivering that crucial blow
When the pain starts to hurt
And you want to go berserk
You think about the many soldiers
Who have fought before
You travel on with winning desire
Fighting for freedom settling the score
A soldier is motivated and licensed to kill
One is dedicated to do their job at will
A soldier will fight until the last
Slowingly making their way with a blast
A soldier is training from the break of dawn
Fighting through the long-lost night
Proving to this hatred world
The American soldier knows how to fight.

SECOND PLATOON'S MOTTO

Second platoon the awesome bunch
Move aside or we will put you in a crunch
We are the best and we know we're good
Because we were trained at Fort Leonard Wood
Tip, top condition you can bet
With Sgts. Strozier, Martin and Leggette
1st and 3rd we carry their slack
That's why they always march in the back
They think they are bad
A bunch of goons
That's why they will never
Make Honor Platoon
Right on second, right on.
"Ruf."
By Second Platoon of Echo 4-4

ROTC

U.S. Anny
Fort Leonard Wood, Missouri
ROTC
All schools should have a military training course,
Reserves Officers Training Corps that gives students a head
Start on their careers.
A military training course in school would give
Students an idea of what the Armed Forces is about.
This could let them know about the Armed Forces'
Fun, excitement, challenges and most of all the
Hard work they will encounter
Therefore, I believe this would give students an idea
Of whether or not they are Uncle Sam's material.
ROTC should be required in all
Schools for it would give students an idea of what
Military life is all about with its demanding
Training program for the conditioning of a complete man.
Most importantly a military training course in
School will be a rewarding learning experience for students
Because they can learn about the pride in serving their country.

ECHO COMPANY'S MOTTO

Weare Echo
Weare mean
Our blood is red
Our clothes are green
Rough and tough
Lean and mean
We are the Army's fighting machine
Echo Company Sergeant
Bayonet training Sergeant.
Shoot to kill!
ByEcho4-4
U.S. Army
Fort Leonard Wood, Missouri

STRONG LOVE

(Based on a true story)

Characters:

Veronica Watson -A beautiful seventeen years old black girl that is slightly mentally retarded. She is a prostitute and drug addict. She is fatherless and is the only child.

A vis Watson -Mother of Veronica. She is a white bisexual, who is a lesbian and prostitute. She is also an alcoholic and drug addict.

Ralph Johnson -A twenty-five years old pimp.

Susan Watson -Grandmother of Veronica. S~e is a 79 years old white woman. She is a nice, caring person. ,

Jack Jones -A client of Avis.

Dr. Hill - Doctor of Veronica

Jimmy Addison -Nurse of Veronica and also her husband.

ACT 1

The weather was extremely cold for there was a blizzard outside on this cold dark lonely night. On Saturday evening at 7 p.m. September 181986 in downtown St. Louis, Missouri in the city projects o public housing, Veronica was watching television alone and waiting for her mother to return home. Ten minutes later Avis enters the apartment.

Avis: (She is drunk and seems to be upset.) Veronica, what are you doing?

Veronica: Nothing Mom.

A vis: I thought I told you to get dressed for the movies! Veronica, I made eighty dollars today by screwing this lesbian. (Veronica's facial expression is one of disappointment. Avis stomps her feet.) I must have privacy tonight because my honey is coming over!

Veronica: (Shouts) Who is it, a lady or a man? (Crying) Momma, are your friends-more important than me?

Avis: (In rage, so she picks up a chair and smashes it across Veronica'shead.)You dam right, rny friends are more irnportant than you.

Veronica: Mom I don't want to go to the movies, all I want is to spend some time with you and watch some television together. (Pleading)

Avis: (She is angry.) Do as I say child. Now get the fuck out of here and find a lover!

Veronica: (Weeping as she is leaving) Mom, have fun.

Avis: Get out of here! (Veronica leaves.)

Veronica went to the movies and on her way back home, she was raped by a psychopath infected with herpes and became pregnant. She was frightened and emotionally drained. She continued on home.

Veronica: (She arrives home and turns the door knob, but it does not open. She hears the stereo playing, so she knocks repeatedly and shouts:) Morn, please let me in! Morn, I have been raped! Mom, Mom, Momma I am scared! Please let me in Mom, I am cold! Momma pretty please let me in! I love you Mom.

Avis and Jack heard the banging on the door, but ignored the noise because they were too involved in their lovemaking.

Jack: Honey, maybe you should open the door to see what she wants.

A vis: (Upset) No, I refuse to open the door, I don' tfeel like being bothered! What is most important, us or that whore at the door?

Jack: We are more important. I love you.

Avis: I love you!

They kiss and continue in their romance, refusing to open the door.

ACT2

Veronica gives up on getting her mother's attention and goes to her grandmother's house.

Veronica: (Arrives at grandmother's house and knocks repeatedly) Grandma please let me in! This is Veronica, your granddaughter! Grandma, please let me in!

Susan: (She is awakened and gets up.) Wait a minute! (Veronica continues on banging on the door, so she gets dressed and opens the door.) What happened to you? Are you alright! (She is shocked.)

Veronica explained what happened and her grandmother with a saddened heart tells her that everything will be okay.

Susan: Veronica, you can stay here with me. Get washed up child and come to bed.

Veronica spent the night with her grandmother then returns home the following day. In the hallway, she sees one of Momma's clients coming of their apartment.

Veronica: (Knocks on the door and enters. Once in, she sees her suitcases packed.) Good morning, Momma. How are you doing this morning? Why are my suitcases packed?

Avis: I must send you to boarding school because my lover Ralph wants to move in. I love him and he loves having sex with me. Veronica you are a woman, I think that you are capable of taking care of yourself. (She grabs Veronica by the hand and carries her suitcases to the door; she opens the door and puts her suitcases in the hall.) I am sorry that I had you and I don't want you in my house anymore because you are occupying space. (Angry) I do not want to see your dumb ass a:gain! You must leave because you are making business bad for me! (She slams the door in Veronica's face.)

Veronica: (Weeping, screaming and banging on the door) But Mom I love you! I am sorry Momma, I never meant to be a pest! Momma Momma please let me in! Mom you think that screwing around with every Tom, Dick and Harry is more important than your daughter!

Avis: (In rage) Get the fuck out of my life you whore!

Veronica stayed there for two hours pleading to her mother for forgiveness. She realizes there is no hope, so she left for her grandmother's house. She arrives safely and Susan lets her in. She explains to her grandmother what had happened. Susan is angry and shocked.

Susan: (Confused) I do not know what is wrong with my daughter! I think that she might be losing her mind. Veronica, you can stay here anytime you want to. My home is your home.

Veronica: Thank you, ma'am, Grandma! (She watched television for seven hours.)

Susan is not feeling very well and she is physically exhausted, so she,goes back to bed. Veronica has a flashback causing her to become upset and depressed. She feels unwanted and believes that no one loves her. She attempts suicide by taking a whole bottle of aspirin. She is unsuccessful because she did not take enough. Her grandmother awakes and checks on her granddaughter, only to find her unconscious. She shakes and tries to revive Veronica. She calls the ambulance. She continues on trying to revive her. The ambulance arrives and takes Veronica to the hospital.

She stayed there for a week. Not once did her mother visit her. She returns to her grandmother;' s house. She is constantly worrying about her mother. Susan suggests to her that she needs to go and enjoy life and stop worrying about Avis.

Veronica: Grandma, could I go to the movies?

Susan: Go right ahead child.

ACT3

Veronica now goes out regularly. One night on her way home, she is approached by this handsome, neatly dressed, twenty-five years old, black man.

Ralph: Hello, beautiful! My name is Ralph Johnson and I am an executive that supervises eight representatives who work for me. I have an opening in my business and I am looking for a sexy body like yours to fill the position. I will make you rich, if you work for my enterprise.

Veronica: What's happening cutie? My name is Veronica Wat son. (She extends her hand and they shake hands.) Gee (excited) oh yes, I would like to be rich! When can I start!

Ralph: You could start as soon as possible. Come with me and I will explain the details.

Veronica: (Agrees) Okay, let's go.

They go into a bar and discuss her new job. Veronica excuses herself and goes to the powder room. While she is gone he puts some Spanish Fly in her drink. They continue talking about the job description. She becomes horny, so he takes her to his place and makes love to her. They spent the entire night together.

Ralph: You were great! Did you enjoy your first time? (Gives her $100) Do you wantto be mature? If so then please take this joint!

Veronica: (Takes the joint) Thank you. I enjoyed tonight.

Ralph: (Persuasively) You could get$100or$200 a night and still have fun. So do you want the job or not?

Veronica: (Thrilled) Yes, Mr. Johnson I want the job. When can I work again?

Ralph: (Pleased) Tonight! Meet me at Frank's Place.

Veronica: I will be there!

Veronica returns home.

Susan: (Worried) Where have you been?

Veronica: Grandma, I have been working at my new job with Johnson Enterprises.

Susan: (Happy) That's good honey. When do you work?

Veronica: Every night and I get paid $100 to $200 a night.

Susan: (Curious) What type of work do you do?

Veronica: I am a representative and my job is to make tourists happy.

Susan: (Excited and proud) You are a smart girl. Get ready for school.

Veronica gets dressed for school and leaves. Her grandmother goes back to bed to rest her painful body. This lifestyle continues for three weeks.

ACT4

Ralph calls her up for some ~ex. Veronica goes over to his place. They get undressed and Ralph realizes that her stomach is big and she must be pregnant. He beats her and shoots her in the stomach. Ralph calls the ambulance and leaves her unconscious. Susan is notified and begins to worry. She rushes to the hospital. Susan stayed in the hospital every day until Veronica begins feeling better. She sees the doctor.

Susan: (Worried) Are you the doctor of Veronica Watson?

Dr Hill: Yes, lam Veronica's doctor. She is instable condition and she will be all right if she stays away from stress. She was abused and shot by a pimp in her stomach. The gunshot blow to the stomach killed her fetus. We did an autopsy of the fetus and we found that the fetus was infected with the herpes virus. We ran tests on her for the herpes virus and they came up negative. We removed the bullet and operated on her to repair her tom flesh. She is conscio.us at this present, so you are welcome to go in.

Susan: (Feeling guilty) I am sorry that this happened. I love you Veronica.

Veronica: Grandma, it is going to be okay. I learned my lesson. I love you Grandma.

Her grandmother stayed there all day long every day until her condition improves. After her condition improves, her Mom visits daily for a couple of hours. While in the hospital she falls in love with her nurse Jimmy, and he falls in love with her. They talk constant! y about a variety of subjects. After two months, she is finally going home.

Jimmy: I love you, Veronica and I have enjoyed taking care of you these past two months. I know what you have experienced and I am willing to help you. I would like for our relationship to grow.

Veronica: I love you Jimmy and you have made my recovery so easy. I am changed and I would like to start a new life with you. I want you to come and visit me.

They kiss and Veronica leaves.

They see each other regularly. Their relationship grows and Veronica solves all of her problems. Jimmy leads her to Christ and she gets saved. They go to a restaurant and have dinner together and later return home.

Jimmy: (Kneeling) Veronica, my father wants you to work for him.

Veronica: (Surprised) Tell your father I accept his offer.

Jimmy: (Still kneeling) Veronica, would you please marry me?

Veronica: (Happy) Oh yes honey, I will marry you (they kiss) but first must ask my grandmother.

Susan: (Eavesdropping, so she heard the good news; therefore, she enters the living room and says:) I give you my permission to marry Jimmy.

They get married and have a successful marriage.

The End

MISTREATED

Hard work is what it takes to succeed in this world
Nobody knows this better than Themlina, the hammer
She is overworked and underpaid
She is used and even abused.
When do you get a lunch break?
Themlina replied, I never get a lunch break
I sometimes work all day without a milkshake.
How do you feel about being abused by careless
Children and adults?
She replied, It's painful and sometimes bothersome.
What are you used as?
She replied, I have been used as a knife,
Wirecutter, sledgehammer, glasscutter to cut glass.
Have you ever been used to complete dangerous jobs?
She replied, Yes, I was once used as a wirecutter
To cut dangerous electrical wires.
Have you ever been left in the rain?
Themlina replied, Yes, I have been left in the rain,
Sleet, snow, electrical storms and frost.
In conclusion Themlina said, I sometimes cry
Because of being overworked and abused
Children and adults don't give me any respect
They treat me like a time fuse.

THE KEY TO LIFE

The key to life is to be an advertising agent
And sell yourself to the "World.

BEING SUCCESSFUL

The key to being successful isn't always
Who you know or what you know
But the key always is who knows you.

INDIVIDUALISM-BEING YOURSELF

When a person believes in individuality
He strongly believes that his concepts,
Ideas, and style are important.
Self-trust is when we trust in ourself
Because society will not trust you.
To show individualism one would do what one wants
' Talk to whosoever one desires to
And also say whatever one feels is right.
A person that shows individualism isn't
Bothered by what society says, does or thinks.
Society is a joint-stock company
In which its members agree
For the better securing of the bread
To each of the shareholders
To surrender the culture of the free.
Stand up for what
You believe is right
Jesus paid the price
And he is our true light.

YOUR CONSCIENCE

If a person doesn't do what is right
His conscience would bother him
Therefore he wouldn't
Be able to sleep at night.
Your conscience guides you
It tells you what is right
And what is wrong.
Let your conscience be your guide
You should obey it
Because it is strong.
And it will not lead you wrong.
Sometimes if a person does something
One is sorry for
Their conscience will cause them to have
Relapses about their wrong-doings.
Your conscience is your guide
It will whip you
If you don't abide.

DEBBIE'S NIGHTMARE

She is a seventeen years old beauty. She is a talented and gifted student. She has won a scholarship to attend Harvard. The bad news is that she will be unable to accept the scholarship because of ten minutes of pleasure. Debbie is the mother of a two weeks old baby. She will not be attending college and might be unable to complete high school because she has a child to care for. Girls and boys, it is natural to want to have sex, but we must make sure that it is safe sex. If we fail to have safe sex, we will be stuck with the financial and psychological burden of raising a child for eighteen years.

If you decide to have sexual intercourse please use the proper contraceptives, so that we can prevent unwanted pregnancy. When a teenager bears a child, the boy and girl are held responsible for feeding and taking care of that child. These teenagers are usually unable to take care of their responsibility; therefore, the burden of care for the baby falls on their parents, which usually causes financial difficulties and family problems. Because of this huge responsibility of caring for a child, these teenagers' career goals now become their second priority. About99 percent (based on a survey of 300 teenaged fathers and mothers) of these boys and girls who are held responsible for a child never become successful.

For thes' teenagers to be successful we must eliminate teenage pregnancy. If you have questions about teenage pregnancy call me at 803-252-6657 or 803-567-4201. You can write me at Route 1 Box 75, Pineville, S.C. 29468 or P.O. Box 83047, University of South Carolina, Columbia, S.C. 29225.

DRUGS AND ALCOHOL- THE SILENT KILLERS

Drugs and alcohol are a dead end. It will leave you all alone without friends. Do not listen to a fool that tells you what is good for your body. Drugs and alcohol are not cool, it is only done by fools. Don't use drugs or alcohol because you will lose control of yourself. Why can't you be like the majority and get a natural high by being successful in life. If you use drugs or alcohol you are committing a slow suicide. If you are an alcoholic or an addict, call or write me: I can help you. You can call me at 803-567-4201 or 803-252-6657. You can write me at P.O. Box 83047, U.S.C., Columbia, S.C. 29225 or Route 1 Box 75, Pineville, S.C. 29468.

SUICIDE

There is no life for me Everything goes wrong and nothing is right.

This is a feeling that we have all experienced at one time or another. We all want to be loved by someone. We sometimes feel that life is not worth living because it seems that no one loves us. I have experienced this state of mind before and I have learned that the best medicine is to have someone to talk to. If anyone is feeling depressed and needs someone to talk to, call or write me. I can help you. You can call me at 803-567-4201or803-252-6657. You can write me at my work address P.O. Box 83047, U.S.C., Columbia, S.C. 29225 or at my home address Route 1 Box 75, Pineville, S.C. 29468.

I believe in hard work
To make an honest living in life.
I remember helping my grand-uncle pick cotton
I worked during the summer
In the cotton and soybeans fields.
I broked corn, picked cucumbers, beans, peas,

Okra, tomatoes, sugar canes, cabbage, rape,
Mustards, turnips and watermelons.
I cropped tobacco and I digged sweet potatoes
And peanuts, I also plowed all of these crops
I worked in a warehouse as a stack boy.
I worked all of these $5 a day jobs
To help pay for some of our family's necessities.

MY LIFE AS IT IS NOW

I was an honor graduate from St. Stephen High
I made a 3.0 my second semester as a freshman
At the University of South Carolina.
I was respected by state officials as one
Of the hardest working Senate Pages in history
This past summer I completed my training
By maxing out in Advanced Individual Training, Physical
Readiness Test and Basic Training at Fort
Leonard Wood, Missouri- U.S. Army.
So as you can see hard work
Is what it takes to be successful.
The Lord spoke to me one day
And he told me a mission that
He wanted me to do.
He said, write poems spreading it over the world
That Jesus Christ loves you.

Made in the USA
Columbia, SC
09 June 2024